4/26/14
$22.60
1785
BdT
JNF

Different States of Matter

Charlotte Deschermeier

PowerKiDS press.

New York

Published in 2014 by The Rosen Publishing Group, Inc.
29 East 21st Street, New York, NY 1001 0

Photo Credits: © 2003-2013 Shutterstock, Inc.

Library of Congress Cataloging-in-Publication Data

Deschermeier, Charlotte.
  Different states of matter / by Charlotte Deschermeier.
     pages cm. – (Ultimate science: Physical science)
  Includes index.
  ISBN 978-1-4777-6093-2 (library) – ISBN 978-1-4777-6094-9 (pbk.) –
  ISBN 978-1-4777-6095-6 (6-pack)
  1. Matter–Properties–Juvenile literature. 2. Matter–Constitution–Juvenile literature. I. Title.
  QC173.36.S38 2014
  530.4–dc23
                              2013023580

Manufactured in the United States of America

CPSIA Compliance Information: Batch #W14PK4: For Further Information contact Rosen Publishing, New York, New York at 1-800-237-9932

Contents

Defining Matter

Everything around you is matter. It is everywhere you look. The computer on your desk, your favorite soda, the air you breathe, and even your pet hamster are made up of matter. Scientists refer to anything that takes up space as "matter."

Everything on Earth is made of matter. Can you find examples of different kinds of matter in this picture?

Matter can come in many different states. It can be solid, like a telephone. Matter can also be liquid, like the water in a fish bowl. Some matter is in the form of a gas. For example, the **helium** in a balloon, which makes it float, is a colorless gas.

Earth and the Moon, seen here from space, are both made of matter.

Every **planet** in the **universe** has matter. Everything in the world, from the tallest mountain to the deepest ocean, is made of matter. Matter makes up your skin, eyes, hair, and the rest of your body. Matter always surrounds you, no matter where you go or what you do.

How Matter Is Formed

Tiny **particles** called **atoms** make up matter. Every solid, liquid, and gas in the universe has atoms. Atoms are so small you cannot see them.

Atoms consist of three parts. These parts are protons, neutrons, and electrons. The nucleus is in the center of an atom. It is made of protons and neutrons. A neutron has no electric charge. The positively charged protons are kept from pushing away from each other by the neutrons that surround them.

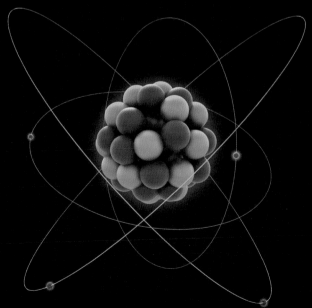

The purple and green neutrons and protons make up the nucleus of this atom. The electrons are the pink balls spinning around the nucleus.

The **negatively** charged electrons move around the nucleus. The electric charges of these three parts help hold an atom together.

Atoms join to form **molecules**. Some molecules, like table salt, are made of only two atoms. Other molecules are larger. For example, a sugar molecule has 45 atoms. Some molecules have many different sorts of atoms. Other molecules have only one kind of atom. Matter made up of only one type of atom is called an element.

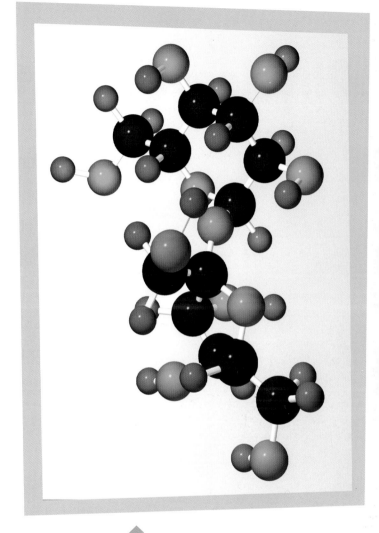

Sucrose molecules, like the one above, have three different types of atoms. Sucrose is another name for table sugar.

Physical Properties of Matter

Every different type of matter has different **physical** properties. Physical properties are things you observe or measure, like size, shape, color, feel, smell, and taste.

Some physical properties you can measure are the **temperatures** at which matter boils, **freezes**, or melts. You can recognize matter by its physical properties. For example, you know that you have been given a chocolate bar if a friend gifts you a present that is hard, thin, rectangular, and smells of chocolate.

Physical properties, like color and smell, allow you to recognize chocolate.

The bowling ball, on the left, and the balloon, are the same size. The bowling ball has a higher density because its molecules are more tightly packed.

An important physical property of matter is mass. The amount of matter in an object is its mass. The mass of an object does not change. Volume is a physical property that tells you how much space a certain object takes up. Scientists use mass and volume to find the **density** of matter. Density tells you how tightly packed molecules are in matter. By **dividing** an object's mass by its volume, you can find its density.

Solids

One of the three most common states of matter is solid. Solids are hard and can keep their shape. Your home, books, and toys are all solid matter.

Molecules stick tightly to each other in solids. Solids cannot change their own shape because their molecules cannot move much. People can change the shape of some solids. You are changing the shape of a stick when you break it into two pieces.

Even if you cut up a cucumber, its volume will always stay the same.

The volume of solids does not change. The two smaller stick pieces take up the same amount of space as the original stick did.

The molecules in a solid are tightly packed together. The density of a solid does not change. For example, you can be sure that your computer will not become soft and drip off your desk. It will maintain its shape.

These marbles are solid. They cannot change shape to fill a jar. They leave empty space between themselves.

Liquids

Another common state of matter is liquid. Liquids do not have a shape of their own, and they can move and flow. Some liquids, like lemonade, move easily. Other liquids, like maple syrup, move slowly. Maple syrup is a thick, sweet liquid made from the sap of maple trees.

Water is an important liquid. Since your body is mostly made up of water, you need to drink it everyday.

You can pour liquids, such as orange juice. This is because the molecules in a liquid slide over each other easily.

Our things, such as clothes and dishes, are also cleaned using water. Many liquids you drink, such as milk, juice, and soda, have water in them.

The molecules in a liquid are not stuck together. Liquid molecules move and take the shape of any **container**. Even though a liquid's shape may change, its volume does not. For example, if you pour a can of soda into a tall, thin glass, the soda's volume remains the same. Only the shape of this liquid is different now.

These glasses hold the same volume of orange juice, even though their shapes are different.

Gases

Gas is the third common state of matter. Like liquids, gases do not have a certain shape. A gas can change its shape to fit the container in which it is placed. Gases are used for many things. You breathe in oxygen gas and breathe carbon dioxide gas. Some houses use natural gas for cooking and heating. Gases such as nitrogen and ammonia are used to make fertilizer. Farmers use fertilizer to help crops grow.

The molecules in a gas are always moving. Gas molecules keep bumping off each other and off the walls of the container that holds them.

You cannot see natural gas, but you can see the flames it makes when it burns.

It is possible for the density of a gas to change. If you pop a helium balloon, the helium molecules will spread out in the room. The density, or how close together the helium molecules are, will go down. If gas is moved from a large container to a smaller one, the density of the gas goes up.

You breathe out the gases carbon dioxide and water vapor. Water vapor is water in the form of a gas.

Changing States of Matter

Matter is able to change its state. For example, a solid ice cube can change into water. Water can also turn into a gas, called water vapor. Temperature changes can cause matter to change its state. Water becomes a solid when its temperature drops below 32° F (0° C). If you raise the temperature of water till it boils, water turns into gas.

If it becomes warm enough, a solid ice cube will melt into a liquid puddle of water.

Chocolate becomes liquid when you melt it. Then you can pour it on ice cream!

Changes in **pressure** can also change the state of matter. Propane gas, which is used in gas grills, becomes a liquid when it is pressed into a container. The pressure in the tank pushes the gas molecules together until they form a liquid.

When matter changes state, its physical properties change. This allows matter to be used in different ways. For example, when solid chocolate melts, you can pour it on ice cream. Matter can change back to its original state. When melted chocolate cools, it will become solid again.

The Kinetic Theory of Matter

Tiny particles make up all matter. Scientists think that the particles in matter are always moving. This idea is called the **kinetic theory** of matter.

Particles in a solid are close together. They vibrate, or move back and forth, a very small amount. You cannot feel it, but the particles in this book are vibrating. The particles in solids are usually closer together than the particles in liquids.

When water boils, its molecules begin to move so quickly that they become a gas.

It is possible for liquid particles to move away from each other. Particles in gases have an even greater distance between them. They move very fast and fill empty spaces near them. Some air molecules travel faster than 1,800 miles per hour (2,897 km/h)!

When matter is heated, its particles move faster. The higher the temperature, the faster the molecules travel. Different types of matter have different-sized particles. Heavier particles move slower than lighter particles at the same temperature.

These water molecules are evaporating. This means the fastest-moving molecules are breaking loose and becoming the gas water vapor.

Scientific Instruments Used to Study Matter

It is easy to see and observe most types of matter, such as solids and liquids. Some gases, like oxygen and helium, cannot be seen. Nor can you see the atoms that make up all matter. This is because atoms are too small to see. Scientists need special instruments to look at and study these tiny pieces of matter.

Scientists use certain kinds of **microscopes** to see atoms. They can see how atoms are arranged in matter using an electron microscope.

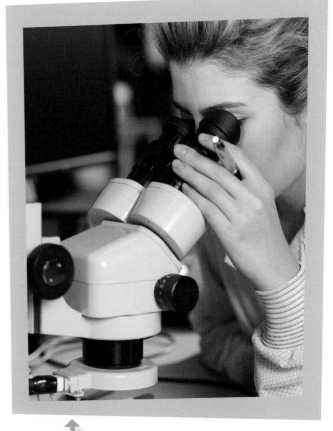

This scientist is using an electron microscope to study matter.

The shape and surface of an atom can be seen with the help of another microscope, called a scanning tunneling microscope. These microscopes help scientists learn about atoms.

Scientists use a balance to measure the amount of mass in a certain piece of matter. The first step in using a balance is to zero the scale. To do this, scientists place an empty cup on the balance and set the scale to zero. The balance will then show you the mass of the matter you place in the cup.

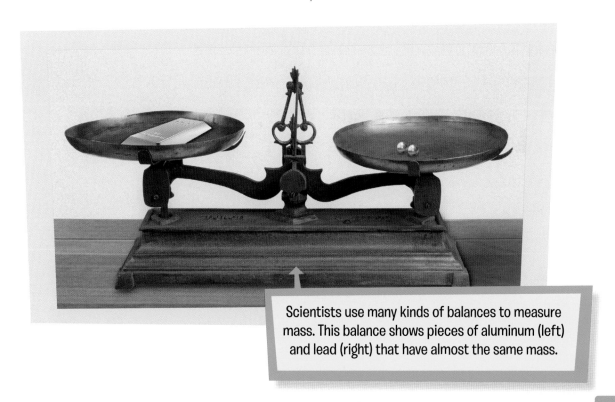

Scientists use many kinds of balances to measure mass. This balance shows pieces of aluminum (left) and lead (right) that have almost the same mass.

Other States of Matter

The three most common states of matter are solids, liquids, and gases. However, scientists have also discovered other kinds of matter. Plasma is a state of matter found at very high temperatures or low pressures. Plasma conducts electricity. Flat TV screens use plasmas. Another type of matter, Bose-Einstein condensate, was discovered in 1995. BEC, as it is known, forms at the coldest temperature scientists can create. Atoms placed in this temperature form one large BEC atom. BEC lasts for only a few minutes.

You use all kinds of matter every day. You need solid food to eat, air to breathe, and water to drink. Most of the Sun is made of plasma. We would not be able to live without the different states of matter.

Glossary

atoms (A-temz) The smallest parts of elements that can exist either alone or with other elements.

container (kun-TAY-ner) Something that holds things.

density (DEN-seh-tee) The heaviness of an object compared to its size.

dividing (dih-VY-ding) To find out the number of times one number goes into another number.

freezes (FREEZ-ez) Makes something so cold it becomes solid.

helium (HEE-lee-um) A light, colorless gas.

kinetic theory (kuh-NEH-tik THEE-uh-ree) The idea that the particles in matter are always moving.

microscopes (MY-kruh-skohps) Instruments used to see very small things.

molecules (MAH-lih-kyoolz) Two or more atoms joined together.

negatively (NEH-guh-tiv-lee) The opposite of positively.

particles (PAR-tih-kulz) Small pieces of matter.

physical (FIH-zih-kul) Having to do with natural forces.

planet (PLA-net) A large object, such as Earth, that moves around the Sun.

pressure (PREH-shur) A force that pushes on something.

temperatures (TEM-pur-cherz) How hot or cold things are.

universe (YOO-nih-vers) All of space.

Index

A
atom(s), 6-7, 20-22

D
density, 9, 11, 15

E
electron microscope, 20
electrons, 6-7

G
gas(es), 5-6, 14-16, 19, 22

L
liquid(s), 5, 12-14, 16-18, 20, 22

M
mass, 9, 21
molecule(s), 7, 9-11, 13-15, 17, 19

N
neutron(s), 6
nucleus, 6-7

P
particles, 6, 18-19
pressure(s), 17, 22
protons, 6

S
scanning tunneling microscope, 21
solid(s), 5-6, 10-11, 16-18, 20, 22

V
volume, 9, 11, 13

Websites

Due to the changing nature of Internet links, PowerKids Press has developed an online list of websites related to the subject of this book. This site is updated regularly. Please use this link to access the list:

www.powerkidslinks.com/usps/states/